SCRAP Crochet 2013
CALENDAR

Annie's™

ScrapCrochet CALENDAR 2013™

Jan

Sun	Mon	Tue	Wed	Thu	Fri	Sat
Dec 30	Dec 31	1 New Year's Day	2	3	4	5
6	7	8	9	10	11	12
13	14	15	16	17	18	19
20	21 Martin Luther King Jr. Day	22	23	24	25	26
27	28	29	30 ●	31	Feb 1	Feb 2

DECEMBER 2012

S	M	T	W	T	F	S
						1
2	3	4	5	6	7	8
9	10	11	12	13	14	15
16	17	18	19	20	21	22
23	24	25	26	27	28	29
30	31					

FEBRUARY 2013

S	M	T	W	T	F	S
					1	2
3	4	5	6	7	8	9
10	11	12	13	14	15	16
17	18	19	20	21	22	23
24	25	26	27	28		

Feb

SCRAP Crochet CALENDAR 2013™

Sun	Mon	Tue	Wed	Thu	Fri	Sat
Jan 27	Jan 28	Jan 29	Jan 30	Jan 31	1	2 Groundhog Day
3	4	5	6	7	8	9
10	11	12	13	14 Valentine's Day	15	16
17	18 Presidents Day	19	20	21	22	23
24	25	26	27 ●	28	Mar 1	Mar 2

JANUARY 2013

S	M	T	W	T	F	S
		1	2	3	4	5
6	7	8	9	10	11	12
13	14	15	16	17	18	19
20	21	22	23	24	25	26
27	28	29	30	31		

MARCH 2013

S	M	T	W	T	F	S
					1	2
3	4	5	6	7	8	9
10	11	12	13	14	15	16
17	18	19	20	21	22	23
24	25	26	27	28	29	30
31						

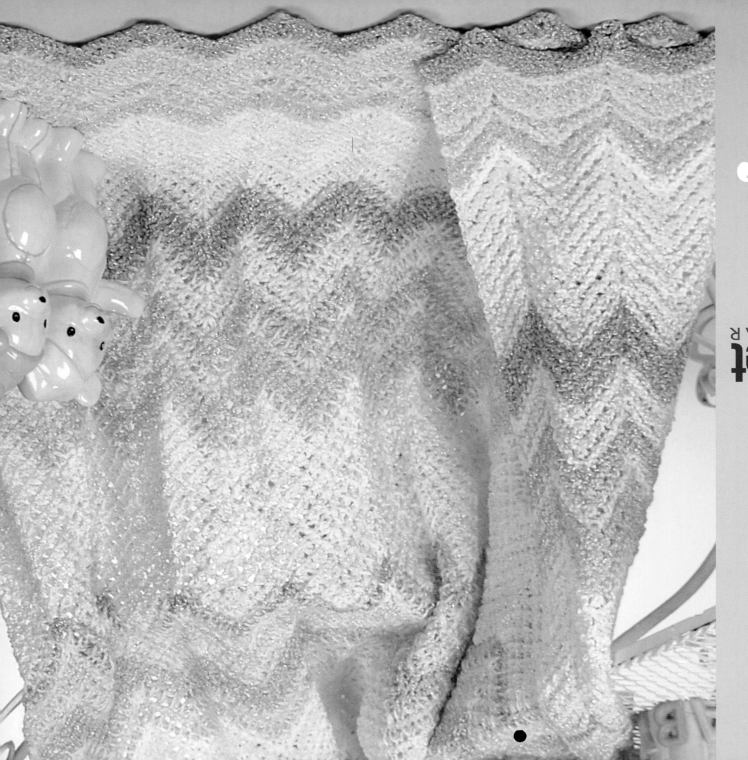

SCRAP Crochet CALENDAR 2013 ™

Sun	Mon	Tue	Wed	Thu	Fri	Sat
Feb 24	**Feb 25**	Feb 26	Feb 27	Feb 28	1	2
3	4	5	6	7	8	9
10 Daylight Saving Time Begins	11	12	13	14	15	16
17 St. Patrick's Day	18	19	20 First Day of Spring	21	22	23
24 Palm Sunday	25	26	27 ●	28	29 Good Friday	30
31 Easter						

FEBRUARY 2013

S	M	T	W	T	F	S
					1	2
3	4	5	6	7	8	9
10	11	12	13	14	15	16
17	18	19	20	21	22	23
24	25	26	27	28		

APRIL 2013

S	M	T	W	T	F	S
	1	2	3	4	5	6
7	8	9	10	11	12	13
14	15	16	17	18	19	20
21	22	23	24	25	26	27
28	29	30				

SCRAP Crochet CALENDAR 2013 ™

Apr

Sun	Mon	Tue	Wed	Thu	Fri	Sat
Mar 31	1 April Fool's Day	2	3	4	5	6
7	8	9	10	11	12	13
14	15	16	17	18	19	20
21	22	23	24	25	26	27
28	29	30	May 1 ●	May 2	May 3	May 4

MARCH 2013

S	M	T	W	T	F	S
					1	2
3	4	5	6	7	8	9
10	11	12	13	14	15	16
17	18	19	20	21	22	23
24	25	26	27	28	29	30
31						

MAY 2013

S	M	T	W	T	F	S
			1	2	3	4
5	6	7	8	9	10	11
12	13	14	15	16	17	18
19	20	21	22	23	24	25
26	27	28	29	30	31	

Sun	Mon	Tue	Wed	Thu	Fri	Sat
Apr 28	Apr 29	Apr 30	1	2	3	4
5	6	7	8	9	10	11
12 Mother's Day	13	14	15	16	17	18
19	20	21	22	23	24	25
26	27 Memorial Day	28	29 ●	30	31	Jun 1

APRIL 2013

S	M	T	W	T	F	S
	1	2	3	4	5	6
7	8	9	10	11	12	13
14	15	16	17	18	19	20
21	22	23	24	25	26	27
28	29	30				

JUNE 2013

S	M	T	W	T	F	S
						1
2	3	4	5	6	7	8
9	10	11	12	13	14	15
16	17	18	19	20	21	22
23	24	25	26	27	28	29
30						

SCRAP Crochet

CALENDAR

2013 ™

Sun	Mon	Tue	Wed	Thu	Fri	Sat
May 26	May 27	May 28	May 29	May 30	May 31	1
2	3	4	5	6	7	8
9	10	11	12	13	14 Flag Day	15
16 Father's Day	17	18	19	20	21 First Day of Summer	22
23	24	25	26 •	27	28	29
30						

MAY 2013

S	M	T	W	T	F	S
			1	2	3	4
5	6	7	8	9	10	11
12	13	14	15	16	17	18
19	20	21	22	23	24	25
26	27	28	29	30	31	

JULY 2013

S	M	T	W	T	F	S
	1	2	3	4	5	6
7	8	9	10	11	12	13
14	15	16	17	18	19	20
21	22	23	24	25	26	27
28	29	30	31			

Jul

2013 ™

Scrap Crochet Calendar

Sun	Mon	Tue	Wed	Thu	Fri	Sat
Jun 30	1	2	3	4 Independence Day	5	6
7	8	9	10	11	12	13
14	15	16	17	18	19	20
21	22	23	24	25	26	27
28	29	30	31 ●	Aug 1	Aug 2	Aug 3

ScrapCrochet
CALENDAR
2013™

Aug

Sun	Mon	Tue	Wed	Thu	Fri	Sat
Jul 28	Jul 29	Jul 30	Jul 31	1	2	3
4	5	6	7	8	9	10
11	12	13	14	15	16	17
18	19	20	21	22	23	24
25	26	27	28 •	29	30	31

JULY 2013

S	M	T	W	T	F	S
	1	2	3	4	5	6
7	8	9	10	11	12	13
14	15	16	17	18	19	20
21	22	23	24	25	26	27
28	29	30	31			

SEPTEMBER 2013

S	M	T	W	T	F	S
1	2	3	4	5	6	7
8	9	10	11	12	13	14
15	16	17	18	19	20	21
22	23	24	25	26	27	28
29	30					

sep

SCRAP Crochet 2013™
CALENDAR

Sun	Mon	Tue	Wed	Thu	Fri	Sat
1	2 Labor Day	3	4	5	6	7
8 National Grandparents Day	9	10	11	12	13	14
15	16	17	18	19	20	21
22 First Day of Autumn	23	25	25	26	27	28
29	30	Oct 1	Oct 2 ●	Oct 3	Oct 4	Oct 5

AUGUST 2013

S	M	T	W	T	F	S
				1	2	3
4	5	6	7	8	9	10
11	12	13	14	15	16	17
18	19	20	21	22	23	24
25	26	27	28	29	30	31

OCTOBER 2013

S	M	T	W	T	F	S
		1	2	3	4	5
6	7	8	9	10	11	12
13	14	15	16	17	18	19
20	21	22	23	24	25	26
27	28	29	30	31		

Sun	Mon	Tue	Wed	Thu	Fri	Sat
Sep 29	Sep 30	1	2	3	4	5
6	7	8	9	10	11	12
13	14 Columbus Day	15	16	17	18	19
20	21	22	23	24	25	26
27	28	29	30 ●	31 Halloween	Nov 1	Nov 2

SEPTEMBER 2013
S M T W T F S
1 2 3 4 5 6 7
8 9 10 11 12 13 14
15 16 17 18 19 20 21
22 23 24 25 26 27 28
29 30

NOVEMBER 2013
S M T W T F S
1 2
3 4 5 6 7 8 9
10 11 12 13 14 15 16
17 18 19 20 21 22 23
24 25 26 27 28 29 30

Sun	Mon	Tue	Wed	Thu	Fri	Sat
Oct 27	Oct 28	Oct 29	Oct 30	Oct 31	1	2
3 Daylight Savings Time ends	4	5 Election Day	6	7	8	9
10	11 Veterans Day	12	13	14	15	16
17	18	19	20	21	22	23
24	25	26	27 ●	28 Thanksgiving Day	29	30

OCTOBER 2013

S	M	T	W	T	F	S
		1	2	3	4	5
6	7	8	9	10	11	12
13	14	15	16	17	18	19
20	21	22	23	24	25	26
27	28	29	30	31		

DECEMBER 2013

S	M	T	W	T	F	S
1	2	3	4	5	6	7
8	9	10	11	12	13	14
15	16	17	18	19	20	21
22	23	24	25	26	27	28
29	30	31				

Sun	Mon	Tue	Wed	Thu	Fri	Sat
1	2	3	4	5	6	7
8	9	10	11	12	13	14
15	16	17	18	19	20	21 First Day of Winter
22	23	24	25 Christmas Day	26	27	28
29	30	31	Jan 1 ●	Jan 2	Jan 3	Jan 4

NOVEMBER 2013

S	M	T	W	T	F	S
					1	2
3	4	5	6	7	8	9
10	11	12	13	14	15	16
17	18	19	20	21	22	23
24	25	26	27	28	29	30

JANUARY 2014

S	M	T	W	T	F	S
			1	2	3	4
5	6	7	8	9	10	11
12	13	14	15	16	17	18
19	20	21	22	23	24	25
26	27	28	29	30	31	

Rippling Waters
Casserole Set

DESIGN BY **DEBORAH LEVY-HAMBURG**

CASSEROLE COZY

SKILL LEVEL ■■■□ INTERMEDIATE

FINISHED SIZE
Fits 9½ x 13½ x 2-inch casserole dish

MATERIALS
- Peaches & Crème medium (worsted) weight cotton yarn (2½ oz/122 yds/71g per ball): 6 balls each #01116 denim blue and #01003 cream
- Size Q/16mm crochet hook or size needed to obtain gauge
- Stitch markers

4 MEDIUM

GAUGE
3 sc = 2 inches; 4 sc rows = 3 inches

PATTERN NOTES
Roll cream and denim blue yarns into 8 balls each.

Hold 8 strands together as 1 throughout.

Do not join rounds unless otherwise stated.

Mark first stitch of each round.

Join with slip stitch as indicated unless otherwise stated.

BOTTOM
Row 1: With **8 strands** cream **held together** (*see Pattern Notes*), ch 9, sc in 2nd ch from hook, sc in each ch across, turn. (*8 sc*)

Row 2: Ch 1, sc in each st across, turn.

Rows 3–15: Rep row 2. At end of last row, do not turn or fasten off.

SIDES
Rnd 1: Working in rnds and in ends of rows, sk first row, sc in end of each row down side, working in starting ch on opposite side of row 1, 3 sc in first ch, sc in each of the next 6 chs, 3 sc in last ch, sk first row, sc in end of each row down other side, 3 sc in first st of row 15, sc in each of next 6 sts, 3 sc in last st, **join** (*see Pattern Notes*) in beg sc. (*52 sc*)

Continued

Rnd 2: Ch 1, sk first st, sc in next st and in each st around with sc in joining sl st of last rnd, do not join.

Rnd 3: Sk ch 1, sc in next st and in each st around.

Rnd 4: Sc in each of next 15 sts, ch 9, sk next 9 sts, sc in each of next 17 sts, ch 9, sk next 9 sts, sc in each of next 2 sts, join in first st of this rnd, turn. Do not fasten off.

FIRST HANDLE

Row 1: Ch 1, sk sl st, sc in each of next 2 sts, sc in each ch of ch-9, sc in each of next 2 sts, sl st in next st, leaving rem sts unworked, turn. *(14 sts)*

Row 2: Ch 1, sk sl st, sc in each st across, leaving last st unworked, turn. *(12 sc)*

Rows 3–9: Ch 1, sk first st, sc in each st across, turn. *(5 sc at end of last row)*

Row 10: Ch 1, sc in each st across, turn.

Row 11: Ch 1, sc in first st, ch 3, sk next 3 sts, sc in last st, turn.

Row 12: Ch 1, sc in each st and in each ch across. Fasten off.

2ND HANDLE

Row 1: Sk next 11 sts of rnd 4 on Sides, join 8 strands of cream in next st, sc in each of next 2 sts, sc in each ch of ch-9, sc in each of next 2 sts, sl st in next st, turn. *(15 sc)*

Row 2: Ch 1, sk sl st, sc in each st across, leaving last 2 sts unworked, turn. *(12 sc)*

Rows 3–12: Rep rows 3–12 of First Handle.

EDGING

Working around top edge of Casserole Cozy, join 8 strands of denim blue with sc in first st of rem unworked sts on 1 side between Handles, *sc in each st across, working in ends of rows up side of Handle, sk first row, sc in each of next 10 rows, sk next row, working across top of Handle, 2 sc in first st, sc in each of next 3 sts, 2 sc in last st, working in ends of rows down other side of Handle, sk first row, sc in each of next 10 rows, sk next row, rep from * on other side of casserole, join in beg sc. Fasten off.

Working in opening at bottom of First Handle, join 8 strands of denim blue in first st of 9 sk sts on rnd 3, sl st in each of next 8 sts, sl st in side of sc on rnd 4, sl st in each ch on opposite side across ch-9, sl st in side of sc on rnd 4, join in beg sl st. Fasten off.

Rep in opening at bottom of other Handle.

COASTER

FINISHED SIZE
12 inches across

MATERIALS
- Peaches & Crème medium (worsted) weight cotton yarn (2½ oz/122 yds/71g per ball)

4
MEDIUM

  1 ball each #01116 denim blue and #01003 cream
- Size G/6/4mm crochet hook or size needed to obtain gauge

GAUGE
Rnds 1–4 = 4½ inches across

PATTERN NOTES
Join with slip stitch as indicated unless otherwise stated.

Chain-3 at beginning of round counts as first double crochet unless otherwise stated.

SPECIAL STITCHES
Beginning V-stitch (beg V-st): Sl st in next ch sp, ch 4 *(counts as first dc and ch-1)*, dc in same ch sp.

V-stitch (V-st): (Dc, ch 1, dc) in next ch sp.

COASTER
Rnd 1: With denim blue, ch 4, sl st in first ch to form ring, **ch 3** *(see Pattern Notes)*, dc in ring, ch 1, [2 dc in ring, ch 1] 5 times, **join** *(see Pattern Notes)* in 3rd ch of beg ch-3. Fasten off. *(12 dc, 6 ch sps)*

Rnd 2: Join cream in any ch sp, **beg V-st** *(see Special Stitches)* in same ch sp, **fpdc** *(see Stitch Guide)* around each of next 2 sts. *V-st *(see Special Stitches)* in next ch sp, fpdc around each of next 2 sts, rep from * around, join in 3rd ch of beg ch-4. Fasten off.

Rnds 3–11: Working rnds, alternating denim blue and cream, join in any ch sp, beg V-st in same ch sp, fpdc around each st around with V-st in ch sp of each V-st around, join in 3rd ch of beg ch-4. Fasten off.

Granny Square
Tissue Cover

DESIGN BY **DEBORAH LEVY-HAMBURG**

SKILL LEVEL ◖■◻▷ EASY

MATERIALS

- Caron Country medium (worsted) weight yarn (3 oz/185 yds/85g per skein):
  1 skein each #0002 coral lipstick, #0007 naturally and #0003 soft sunshine
- Size H/8/5mm crochet hook or size needed to obtain gauge

GAUGE

2 shells and ch 2 = 2 inches; 5 shell rows = 3 inches

PATTERN NOTES

Chain-3 at beg of round counts as first double crochet unless otherwise stated.

Join with slip stitch as indicated unless otherwise stated.

Continued

SIDE
Make 4.

Rnd 1: With soft sunshine, ch 4, sl st in first ch to form ring, **ch 3** (see Pattern Notes), 2 dc in ring, ch 3 [3 dc in ring, ch 3] 3 times, **join** (see Pattern Notes) in 3rd ch of beg ch 3. Fasten off. (12 dc, 4 ch sps)

Rnd 2: Join coral lipstick in any ch sp, for beginning corner (beg corner), (ch 3, 2 dc, ch 3, 3 dc) in same ch sp, ch 2, *for corner, (3 dc, ch 3, 3 dc) in next ch sp, ch 2, rep from * twice, join in 3rd ch of beg ch-3. (4 corners, 4 ch sps)

Rnd 3: Sl st in each of next 2 sts, sl st in first ch sp, beg corner, ch 2, *for shell, (3 dc, ch 2) in next ch sp, corner, ch 2, rep from * twice, shell, join in 3rd ch of beg ch-3. Fasten off. (4 corners, 4 shells)

Rnd 4: Join naturally in ch sp of beg corner, beg corner, *ch 2, shell in next 2 ch sps to next corner, corner, rep from * twice, ch 2, shell in next 2 ch sps, join in 3rd ch of beg ch-3. Fasten off.

TOP
Rnd 1: With soft sunshine, ch 30, sl st in first ch to form ring, ch 3, 2 dc in ring, ch 1, [3 dc in ring, ch 1] 11 times, join in 3rd ch of beg ch-3. Fasten off. (36 dc, 12 ch sps)

Rnd 2: Join coral lipstick in any ch sp, (ch 3, 2 dc) in same ch sp, ch 1, [3 dc in next ch sp, ch 1] around, join in 3rd ch of beg ch-3. Fasten off.

Rnd 3: Join naturally in any ch sp, beg corner, *ch 2, shell, in next 2 ch sps, corner, rep from * twice, ch 2, shell in next 2 ch sps, join in 3rd ch of beg ch-3. Fasten off.

With naturally, working through both thicknesses, sl st Sides with WS tog to form box. Sl st Top to top edge of Sides.

TRIM
Rnd 1: Join naturally in any ch sp on bottom edge of Sides, (ch 3, 2 dc) in same ch sp, ch 2, shell in each ch sp around, join in 3rd ch of beg ch-3.

Rnd 2: St st in next st, ch 3, dc in next st, dc in next ch sp, [sk next st, dc in each of next 2 sts, dc in next ch sp] around, join in 3rd ch of beg ch-3. Fasten off.

●

March

Rainbow Sherbet Afghan

DESIGN BY **DARLA FANTON**

SKILL LEVEL ●●●◻ INTERMEDIATE

SIZE
36 x 46 inches

MATERIALS
- Bernat Softee Baby light (DK) weight yarn (5 oz/362 yds/ 140 grams per skein):
  - 1 skein #02000 white
  - 7 oz assorted scrap colors
- Size H/8/5mm afghan crochet hook or size needed to obtain gauge
- Tapestry needle

GAUGE
Point to point = 3½ inches; 2 rows = 1 inch

PATTERN NOTES
Each colored row *(consisting of a work-off pass and a pick-up pass)* requires approximately 14 yards.

For the return portion of a row, when you work the next loop off the hook following the chain-3, it actually creates a 4th chain so that on the next row when you skip a chain, pick up a loop in each of the next 2 chains, you will be picking up loops in the center 2 of 4 chains.

Continued

AFGHAN

Row 1:

A. With desired scrap color, ch 244, holding all lps on hook, working in back bar of ch (*see illustration*), pull up lp in 2nd ch from hook, pull up lp in each of the rem chs (244 lps on hook);

Back Bar of Chain

B. yo, pull through first 3 lps on hook, *[yo, pull through 2 lps on hook] 9 times, ch 3, [yo, pull through 2 lps on hook] 9 times, yo, pull through 5 lps (*cl made*), rep from * across, ending with yo, pull through 4 lps on hook (*last cl*), rem lp counts as first st of next row.

Row 2:

A. Holding all lps on hook, ch 1, sk first cl, *pick up lp under next vertical bar, [yo, sk next vertical bar, pick up lp under next vertical bar] 4 times, yo, sk next ch, [pick up lp in next ch] twice, yo, pick up lp under next vertical bar, [yo, sk next vertical bar, pick up lp under next vertical bar] 4 times, sk next cl, rep from * across, ending with pick up lp in top of last cl;

B. rep B as for row 1.

Row 3:

A. Pick up lps as for row 2, noting that the vertical bars you will sk in fact look more diagonal than vertical. Fasten off color.

B. Place white on hook with slip knot, pull slip knot through first 3 lps on hook, *pick up lp under next vertical bar, [yo, sk next vertical bar, pick up lp under next vertical bar] 4 times, yo, sk next ch, [pick up lp in next ch] twice, yo, pick up lp under next vertical bar, [yo, sk next vertical bar, pick up lp under next vertical bar] 4 times, sk next cl, rep from * across, ending with pick up lp in top of last cl.

Row 4:

A. Pick up lps as for row 3, drop white at end of row, but do not fasten off, instead carry along side edge, twisting to avoid holes.

B. Place next scrap color on hook and continue as for row 3.

Row 5: Rep row 2.

Row 6:

A. Rep row 3 to pick up lps;

B. pick up white and work as for row 1.

Row 7: Rep row 4.

Row 8: Rep row 6.

Row 9: Rep row 4.

Row 10: Rep row 2.

Rows 11–91: [Rep rows 2–10 consecutively] 9 times, noting that since you are carrying the white along the side edge, the return portion of row 3 will now be the same as the return for row 6.

Row 92: Rep row 2.

Last row: Bind off in the following manner: Ch 1, sk first cl, *[pick up lp under next vertical bar and pull through lp already on hook] 9 times, [pick up lp in next ch and pull through lp already on hook] 4 times, [pick up lp under next vertical bar and pull through lp already on hook] 9 times, sk cl, rep from * across, ending with pick up lp in top of last cl and pull through lp on hook. Fasten off.

April

Cross Bookmark

DESIGN BY **DIONNE BARRATT**

SKILL LEVEL ■■■□ INTERMEDIATE

FINISHED SIZE
4¼ x 5¾ inches, excluding Tassel

MATERIALS
- Size 10 crochet cotton:
  100 yds white
- Size 7/1.65mm steel crochet hook
  or size needed to obtain gauge

0 LACE

GAUGE
Rnds 1–3 = 1½ inches across

PATTERN NOTES
Chain-3 at beginning of row counts as first
double crochet unless otherwise stated.

Join with slip stitch as indicated unless
otherwise stated.

SPECIAL STITCHES
Beginning cluster (beg cl): Ch 3 (*see Pattern
Notes*), *yo twice, insert hook in same st, yo,
pull lp through, [yo, pull through 2 lps on
hook] twice, rep from * once, yo, pull through
all lps on hook.

Cluster (cl): Yo twice, insert hook in next st,
yo, pull lp through, [yo, pull through 2 lps on
hook] twice, *yo twice, insert hook in same st,

yo, pull lp through, [yo, pull through 2 lps on
hook] twice, rep from * once, yo, pull through
all lps on hook.

Beginning shell (beg shell): Ch 3, (3 dc, ch 3,
4 dc) in same ch sp.

Shell: (4 dc, ch 3, 4 dc) in next ch sp.

Picot: Ch 6, sc in 5th ch from hook.

CROSS
Rnd 1: Ch 2, 8 sc in 2nd ch from hook, **join**
(*see Pattern Notes*) in beg sc. (*8 sc*)

Rnd 2: **Beg cl** (*see Special Stitches*), ch 3, [**cl** (*see
Special Stitches*), ch 3] 7 times, join in top of
beg cl. (*8 cls, 8 ch sps*)

Rnd 3: Sl st in first ch sp, **beg shell** (*see Special
Stitches*), ch 3, sc in next ch sp, ch 3, *shell (*see
Special Stitches*) in next st, ch 3, sc in next ch sp,
ch 3; rep from * around, join in 3rd ch of beg
ch-3. (*8 ch sps, 4 shells, 4 sc*)

FIRST POINT
Row 4: Now working in rows, sl st in each of
next 3 sts, sl st in next ch sp, beg shell, leaving
rem sts unworked, turn. (*1 shell*)

Row 5: Sl st in each of next 3 sts, sl st in next ch
sp, beg shell, turn.

Row 6: Sl st in each of next 3 sts, sl st in next ch
sp, ch 3, (3 dc, **picot**—*see Special Stitches*, 4 dc)
in same ch sp, do not turn. Fasten off.

2ND POINT
Row 4: Join in ch sp of next unworked shell on
rnd 3, beg shell, leaving rem sts unworked, turn.

Rows 5 & 6: Rep rows 5 and 6 of First Point.

3RD POINT
Rep 2nd Point once for a total of 3 Points.

4TH POINT
Row 4: Join in ch sp of last unworked shell on rnd
3, beg shell, leaving rem sts unworked, turn.

Rows 5–10: Rep row 5 of First Point.

Row 11: Rep row 6 of First Point.

TASSEL
Cut 8 strands of thread, each 6 inches long. Cut
a separate strand and tie tightly around middle
of all strands (for tie), fold strands in half. Wrap
another strand 3 times around folded strands
⅜ inch from top of fold, secure and hide ends
inside Tassel. Trim all ends even. Using tie,
attach to picot on 4th Point.

Grape Cluster
Trivets

DESIGNS BY **DEBRA ARCH**

FINISHED SIZE
5 x 6 inches

MATERIALS
- Aunt Lydia's Classic Crochet #10 Cotton 350 yds per ball
  1 ball #458 purple
  1 ball #397 wasabi
- Size 7/1.65mm steel crochet hook or size needed to obtain gauge
- Size C/2/2.75mm crochet hook or size needed to obtain gauge
- Tapestry needle
- Metal bottle caps: 13

GAUGE
Size 7 steel hook: 2 hdc = ¼ inch; 3 hdc rnds = ½ inch

Size C hook: 8 hdc = 1 inch; 2 hdc rows = ⅜ inch

PATTERN NOTES
Chain-2 at beginning of round counts as first half double crochet unless otherwise stated.

Join with slip stitch as indicated unless otherwise stated.

TRIVET
LEAF
MAKE 2.

Rnd 1: With size C hook and wasabi, ch 8, 3 hdc in 2nd ch from hook, hdc in each of next 5 chs, 3 hdc in last ch, working on opposite side of starting ch, hdc in each of next 5 chs, **join**

(see Pattern Notes) in beg hdc. *(16 hdc)*

Rnd 2: Ch 2 *(see Pattern Notes)*, 3 hdc in next st, hdc in each of next 7 sts, 3 hdc in next st, hdc in each of last 6 sts, join in 2nd ch of beg ch-2. *(20 hdc)*

Rnd 3: Ch 1, sl st in each of first 3 sts, *(sc, hdc, dc, tr, dc, hdc, sc) in next st**, sl st in each of next 3 sts, rep from * around, ending last rep at **, join in beg sl st. Fasten off. *(50 sts)*

Continued

GRAPE
MAKE 13.

Rnd 1: Using size 7 hook and purple, ch 2, 10 hdc in 2nd ch from hook, join in beg hdc. (*10 hdc*)

Rnd 2: Ch 2, hdc in same st, 2 hdc in each st around, join in 2nd ch of beg ch-2. (*20 hdc*)

Rnd 3: Ch 2, hdc in same st, hdc in next st, [2 hdc in next st, hdc in next st] around, join in 2nd ch of beg ch-2. (*30 hdc*)

Rnd 4: Working in **back lps** (*see Stitch Guide*), ch 2, hdc in each st around, join in 2nd ch of beg ch-2.

Rnds 5–7: Ch 2, hdc in each st around, join in 2nd ch of beg ch-2. At end of last rnd, leaving long end. Fasten off.

ASSEMBLY
Weave long end in top of sts on last rnd, insert bottle cap with print side down so that it will be top of Grape, pull long end to close. Secure end.

Rep with rem Grapes.

Arrange Grapes as shown in photo and sew tog.

Sew Leaves to top of Grapes as shown in photo.

LARGE TRIVET

SKILL LEVEL ■■□▭ EASY

FINISHED SIZE
10 x 12 inches

MATERIALS
- Peaches and Crème medium (worsted) weight cotton yarn (2½ oz/122 yds/71g per ball): 3 balls #122 grape 1 ball #01084 sage green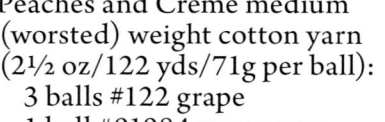
- Size I/9/5.5mm crochet hook or size needed to obtain gauge
- Tapestry needle
- Regular mouth canning jar lids and bands: 8

GAUGE
3 hdc = 1 inch; 2 hdc rnds = 1 inch

PATTERN NOTES
Chain-2 at beginning of round counts as first half double crochet unless otherwise stated.

Join with slip stitch as indicated unless otherwise stated.

INSTRUCTIONS
TRIVET
LEAF
MAKE 2.

Rnd 1: With sage green, ch 8, 3 hdc in 2nd ch from hook, hdc in each of next 5 chs, 3 hdc in last ch, working on opposite side of starting ch, hdc in each of next 5 chs, **join** (*see Pattern Notes*) in beg hdc. (*16 hdc*)

Rnd 2: **Ch 2** (*see Pattern Notes*), 3 hdc in next st, hdc in each of next 7 sts, 3 hdc in next st, hdc in each of next 6 sts, join in 2nd ch of beg ch-2. (*20 hdc*)

Rnd 3: Ch 1, sl st in each of next 3 sts, *(sc, hdc, dc, **fptr**—*see Stitch Guide*, around next st 2 rnds below, dc, hdc, sc) in next st**, sl st in each

of next 3 sts, rep from * around, ending last rep at **, join in beg sl st. Fasten off. (*50 sts*)

GRAPE
MAKE 8.

Rnd 1: Holding 2 strands of grape tog, ch 2, 10 hdc in 2nd ch from hook, join in beg hdc. (*10 hdc*)

Rnd 2: Ch 2, hdc in same st, 2 hdc in each st around, join in 2nd ch of beg ch-2. (*20 hdc*)

Rnd 3: Ch 2, hdc in same st, hdc in next st, [2 hdc in next st, hdc in next st] around, join in 2nd ch of beg ch-2. (*30 hdc*)

Rnd 4: Ch 2, hdc in each st around, join in 2nd ch of beg ch-2.

Rnd 5: Working in **back lps** (*see Stitch Guide*), ch 2, *hdc dec (*see Stitch Guide*) in next 2 sts**, hdc in next st, rep from * around, ending last rep at **, join in 2nd ch of beg ch-2.

Rnd 6: Ch 2, hdc in each st around, join in 2nd ch of beg ch-2. Leaving long end, fasten off.

ASSEMBLY
Weave long end through top of sts on last rnd, insert canning jar lid in first, then insert band, pull long end to close. Secure end.

Rep with rem Grapes.

Arrange Grapes as shown in photo and sew tog.

Sew Leaves to top of Grapes as shown in photo.

Summertime Hat

DESIGN BY **MICKIE AKINS**

SKILL LEVEL  EASY

FINISHED SIZE

One size fits most

MATERIALS

- Peaches & Crème medium (worsted) weight yarn (2½ oz/122 yds/71g per ball): 2 balls #01042 tea rose
- Size G/6/4mm crochet hook or size needed to obtain gauge
- Stitch marker

GAUGE

4 sc = 1 inch; 4 sc rnds = 1 inch

PATTERN NOTES

Work in continuous rounds; do not turn or join rounds unless otherwise stated.

Mark first stitch of each round.

HAT

Rnd 1: Ch 2, 6 sc in 2nd ch from hook, **do not join** (see Pattern Notes). (6 sc)

Rnd 2: 2 sc in each st around. (12 sc)

Continued

Rnd 3: [Sc in next st, 2 sc in next st] around. (*18 sc*)

Rnd 4: [Sc in each of next 2 sts, 2 sc in next st] around. (*24 sc*)

Rnd 5: [Sc in each of next 3 sts, 2 sc in next st] around. (*30 sc*)

Rnd 6: [Sc in each of next 4 sts, 2 sc in next st] around. (*36 sc*)

Rnd 7: [Sc in each of next 5 sts, 2 sc in next st] around. (*42 sc*)

Rnd 8: [Sc in each of next 6 sts, 2 sc in next st] around. (*48 sc*)

Rnd 9: [2 sc in next st, sc in each of next 7 sts] around. (*54 sc*)

Rnd 10: Sc in each of first 4 sts, [2 sc in next st, sc in each of next 8 sts] around to last 5 sts, 2 sc in next st, sc in each of last 4 sts. (*60 sc*)

Rnd 11: Sc in each st around.

Rnd 12: [2 sc in next st, sc in each of next 9 sts] around. (*66 sc*)

Rnd 13: Sc in each of first 5 sts, [2 sc in next st, sc in each of next 10 sts] around to last 6 sts, 2 sc in next st, sc in each of last 5 sts. (*72 sc*)

Rnd 14: [2 sc in next st, sc in each of next 11 sts] around. (*78 sc*)

Rnd 15: Sc in each of first 6 sts, [2 sc in next st, sc in each of next 12 sts] around to last 7 sts, 2 sc in next st, sc in each of last 6 sts, join in beg sc. (*84 sc*)

Rnd 16: [Sc in each of next 13 sts, 2 sc in next st] around. (*90 sc*)

Rnd 17: Ch 1, sc in each of first 7 sts, [2 sc in next st, sc in each of next 14 sts] around to last 8 sts, 2 sc in next st, sc in each of last 7 sts, join in beg sc. (*96 sc*)

Rnds 18–29: Sc in each st around.

Rnd 30: Working in **front lps** (*see Stitch Guide*), [sc in each of next 3 sts, 2 sc in next st] around. (*120 sc*)

Rnds 31 & 32: Working in both lps, sc in each st around.

Rnd 33: [Sc in each of next 4 sts, 2 sc in next st] around. (*144 sc*)

Rnds 34–39: Sc in each st around.

Rnd 40: Sl st in each st around. Fasten off.

Patriotic **Bear**

DESIGN BY **BEVERLY MEWHORTER**

SKILL LEVEL ◖◼◻◻ EASY

FINISHED SIZE
5 inches tall, sitting

MATERIALS
- Fuzzy medium (worsted) weight yarn:
  1½ oz/75 yds/43g white
  ½ oz/25 yds/14g each red and blue
- Size H/8/5mm crochet hook or size needed to obtain gauge
- 10mm animal eyes: 2
- 5mm black round half bead
- 5mm white iridescent star sequins: 9
- Toothpick flag
- Polyester fiberfill
- Craft glue
- Tapestry needle

4 MEDIUM

GAUGE
7 sc = 2 inches; 7 sc rows = 2 inches

PATTERN NOTE
Join with slip stitch as indicated unless otherwise stated.

Continued

BEAR
HEAD

Rnd 1: With white, starting at Head, ch 2, 6 sc in 2nd ch from hook, **join** *(see Pattern Note)* in beg sc. *(6 sc)*

Rnd 2: Ch 1, 2 sc in each st around, join in beg sc. *(12 sc)*

Rnd 3: Ch 1, sc in first st, 2 sc in next st, [sc in next st, 2 sc in next st] around, join in beg sc. *(18 sc)*

Rnds 4–6: Ch 1, sc in each st around, join in beg sc.

Rnd 7: Ch 1, sc in first st, **sc dec** *(see Stitch Guide)* in next 2 sts, [sc in next st, sc dec in next 2 sts] around, join in beg sc. *(12 sc)*

Rnd 8: Ch 1, sc dec in first 2 sts, [sc dec in next 2 sts] around, join in beg sc. Stuff. Continue stuffing as you work. *(6 sc)*

BODY

Rnds 9 & 10: Rep rnds 2 and 3.

Rnd 11: Ch 1, sc in each of first 2 sts, 2 sc in next st, [sc in each of next 2 sts, 2 sc in next st] around, join in beg sc. *(24 sc)*

Rnd 12: Ch 1, sc in each of first 3 sts, 2 sc in next st, [sc in each of next 3 sts, 2 sc in next st] around, join in beg sc. *(30 sc)*

Rnds 13–16: Rep rnd 4.

Rnd 17: Rep rnd 7. *(20 sc)*

Rnd 18: Ch 1, sc in first st, sc dec in next 2 sts, [sc in next st, sc dec in next 2 sts] 6 times, sc in each of last 2 sts, join in beg sc. *(14 sc)*

Rnd 19: Rep rnd 8. Leaving long end for weaving, fasten off. *(7 sc)*

Weave end through sts of last rnd, pull tight to gather. Secure end.

ARMS & LEGS
Make 4.

Rnd 1: With white, ch 2, 8 sc in 2nd ch from hook, join in beg sc. *(8 sc)*

Rnds 2–7: Ch 1, sc in each st around, join in beg sc. At end of last rnd, fasten off. Stuff.

Flatten last rnd, sew Arms to each side of Body over rnds 11–13 and Legs to each side of Body over rnds 15–17 so Bear is sitting as shown in photo.

EAR
Make 2.

With white, ch 2, 7 sc in 2nd ch from hook, do not join. Fasten off.

Sew flat edge of Ears to top of Head spaced ¾ inch apart.

MUZZLE

Rnd 1: With white, ch 2, 8 sc in 2nd ch from hook, join in first sc. *(8 sc)*

Rnd 2: Ch 1, sc in each st around, join in beg sc. Fasten off. Stuff lightly.

Sew to center front of Head over rnds 4–7.

COLLAR

With red, ch 17, sc in 2nd ch from hook, sc in each ch across. Fasten off.

Place Collar around neck of Bear and sew ends tog.

TIE

With blue, ch 15, dc in 4th ch from hook, dc in each of next 2 chs, hdc in each of next 4 chs, sc in each of next 2 chs, sl st in next ch, (sc, hdc) in next ch, 4 dc in last ch; working on opposite side of ch, (hdc, sc) in next ch, sl st in next ch, sc in each of next 2 chs, hdc in each of next 4 chs, dc in each of next 3 chs, ch 3, sl st in last ch. Fasten off.

Wrap blue 3 times around sl sts before and after 4-dc group on top of Tie. Secure.

FINISHING

Glue animal eyes to Head centered above Muzzle ⅜ inch apart.

Glue half round bead to center of Muzzle for nose.

Glue sequins randomly over Tie. Glue top of Tie to Collar.

Insert toothpick flag through one Arm.

Swirly
Hot Pads

DESIGN BY **KATHLEEN GAREN**

SKILL LEVEL  INTERMEDIATE

SIZE
Each Hot Pad is 9 inches across.

MATERIALS
For one hot pad
- Medium (worsted) weight yarn:
  2½ oz/125 yds/71g main color
  (MC)
  10 yds each assorted scrap colors
- Size H/8/5mm crochet hook or size
  needed to obtain gauge
- Stitch marker

4
MEDIUM

GAUGE
Center and rnd 1 of Hot Pad = 3 inches across.

PATTERN NOTES
Do not join rounds unless otherwise stated.

Mark first st of each rnd.

Join with slip stitch as indicated unless
otherwise stated.

SPECIAL STITCH
Cluster (cl): [Yo, insert hook in ring, yo, pull lp
through, yo, pull through 2 lps on hook] twice,
yo, pull through all lps on hook.

Continued

SQUARE HOT PAD

CENTER
Make 2.

With scrap color, ch 5, sl st in first ch to form ring, ch 2, dc in ring, ch 2, **cl** (see Special Stitch) in ring, ch 1, (cl, ch 2, cl, ch 1) 3 times in ring, **join** (see Pattern Notes) in first dc. Fasten off. (4 ch-1 sps, 4 ch-2 sps)

HOT PAD
Rnd 1: Holding Centers with WS tog, matching ch sps and working through both thicknesses, join next scrap color with sc in any ch-1 sp, ch 1, dc in next ch sp, *ch 1, (dc, ch 2, dc) in same sp as last dc, [ch 1, **dc dec** (see Stitch Guide) in same ch sp as last dc and next ch sp] twice rep from * twice, ch 1, (dc, ch 2, dc) in same sp as last dc dec, ch 1, dc dec in same sp as last dc and same ch sp as first sc, ch 1, sk first sc, join in top of next dc. Fasten off. (12 ch-1 sps, 4 ch-2 sps)

Rnd 2: Join MC with sc in any corner ch-2 sp, 2 sc in same ch sp as joining sc, 2 sc in each ch-1 sp and 4 sc in each corner ch-2 sp around, sc in same ch sp as joining sc. (40 sc)

Rnd 3: Work rem rnds in **back lps** (see Stitch Guide), [2 sc in each of next 2 sts, sc in each of next 8 sts] around, **do not join** (see Pattern Notes), **mark first st** (see Pattern Notes). (48 sts)

Rnd 4: [2 sc in next st, sc in each of next 2 sts, 2 sc in next st, sc in each of next 8 sts] around. (56 sts)

Rnd 5: [2 sc in next st, sc in each of next 4 sts, 2 sc in next st, sc in each of next 8 sts around. (64 sts)

Rnd 6: [2 sc in next st, sc in each of next 6 sts, 2 sc in next st, sc in each of next 8 sts] around. (72 sts)

Rnd 7: [2 sc in next st, sc in each of next 8 sts] around. (80 sts)

Rnd 8: Sc in next st, 2 sc in next st, sc in each st around; sc in first 2 sts to finish shaping, join in next st. Fasten off. (81sts)

TOP RIDGES
Working in **front lps** (see Stitch Guide), join MC with sc in first st of rnd 2, sc in each st around rnds 2–8. Fasten off.

EDGING
Rnd 1: Working in back lps of rnd 8, join scrap color with sc in any st, ch 3, dc in same st as sc, sk next 2 sts, *(sc, ch 3, dc) in next st, sk next 2 sts; rep from * around, join in first sc. Fasten off.

Rnd 2: Working behind last rnd, in back lps of sk sts on rnd 8, join next scrap color with sc in 2nd sk st, ch 3, dc in same st as sc, *(sc, ch 3, dc) in 2nd st of next 2 sk sts; rep from * around, join in beg sc. Fasten off.

ROUND HOT PAD

CENTER
Make 2.

With scrap color, ch 5, sl st in first ch to form ring, ch 2, dc in ring, ch 2, (**cl**—see Special Stitch, in ring, ch 2) 6 times, **join** (see Pattern Notes) in first dc. Fasten off. (7 ch-2 sps)

HOT PAD
Rnd 1: Holding Centers with WS tog, matching ch sps and working through both thicknesses, join next scrap color with sc in any ch sp, ch 1, (dc, ch 1, dc) in next ch sp, ch 1, *dc dec (see Stitch Guide) in same ch sp as last dc worked and next ch sp, ch 1, dc in same ch sp last worked in, ch 1; rep from * around, sk first sc, join in next dc. Fasten off. (14 ch-1 sps)

Rnd 2: Join MC with sc in any ch sp, 2 sc in same sp as last sc, 2 sc in next ch sp, [3 sc in next ch sp, 2 sc in next ch sp] around. (35 sts)

Rnd 3: Work rem rnds in **back lps** (see Stitch Guide), [sc in each of next 4 sts, 2 sc in next st] around, **do not join** (see Pattern Notes), **mark first st** (see Pattern Notes). (42 sts)

Rnd 4: Sc in each of next 2 sts, 2 sc in next st, [sc in each of next 5 sts, 2 sc in next st] around to last 3 sts, sc in each of last 3 sts. (49 sts)

Rnd 5: Sc in each of next 6 sts, 2 sc in next st] around. (56 sts)

Rnd 6: Sc in each of next 3 sts, 2 sc in next st, [sc in each of next 7 sts, 2 sc in next st] around to last 4 sts, sc in each of last 4 sts. (63 sts)

Rnd 7: [Sc in each of next 8 sts, 2 sc in next st] around. (70 sts)

Rnd 8: Sc in each of next 4 sts, 2 sc in next st, [sc in each of next 8 sts, 2 sc in next st] around to last 2 sts, sc in each of last 2 sts, working across first sts of this rnd, sc in each of first 3 sts to round out curve, join in next st. Fasten off. (78 sts)

TOP RIDGES
Working in **front lps** (see Stitch Guide), join MC with sc in first st of rnd 2, sc in each st around rnds 2–8. Fasten off.

EDGING
Rnd 1: Working in back lps of rnd 8, join scrap color with sc in any st, ch 3, dc in same st as sc, sk next 2 sts, *(sc, ch 3, dc) in next st, sk next 2 sts; rep from *around, join in first sc. Fasten off.

Rnd 2: Working behind last rnd, in back lps of sk sts on rnd 8, join next scrap color with sc in 2nd sk st, ch 3, dc in same st as sc, *(sc, ch 3, dc) in 2nd st of next 2 sk sts; rep from *around, join in beg sc. Fasten off.

September

Tutti-Frutti

DESIGN BY **SHARON HATFIELD**

SKILL LEVEL ■■□□ EASY

FINISHED SIZE
Adult—one size fits all

MATERIALS
- Red Heart Kids medium (worsted) weight yarn (solids: 5 oz/290 yds/141g; variegated: 4 oz/232 yds/113g per skein):
    1 skein each #2734 pink and #2935 sherbet multi
- Size P/Q/15mm crochet hook or size needed to obtain gauge
- 2-inch-square cardboard
- Tapestry needle

4 MEDIUM

GAUGE
With 2 strands of yarn held tog: 2 hdc = 1 inch; 7 hdc rnds = 5 inches

PATTERN NOTES
Work in continuous rounds, do not join or turn unless otherwise stated. Mark first st of each rnd.

Hold 2 strands together unless otherwise stated.

Join with slip stitch as indicated unless otherwise stated.

FOOT WARMER
Make 2.

Rnd 1: Starting at toe, with sherbet multi, ch 2, 8 hdc in 2nd ch from hook, **do not join** (see Pattern Notes). (8 hdc)

Rnd 2: 2 hdc in each st around.

Rnds 3–12: Hdc in each st around. At end of last rnd, **join** (see Pattern Notes) in first hdc. Fasten off.

Rnd 13: Join pink in first st, ch 2 (counts as first hdc), hdc in each st around, do not join.

Rnds 14–20: Hdc in each st around.

Rnd 21: [Hdc in each of next 3 sts, 2 hdc in next st] around. (20 hdc)

Rnds 22–30: Hdc in each st around. At end of last rnd, join in first hdc. Fasten off.

Rnd 31: For cuff, join sherbet multi in first st, ch 3 (counts as first dc), dc in same st as beg ch-3, dc in next st, [2 dc in next st, dc in next st] around, join in 3rd ch of beg ch-3. (30 dc)

Rnd 32: Ch 3, **fpdc** (see Stitch Guide) around post of next st, ***bpdc** (see Stitch Guide) around post of next st, fpdc around post of next st, rep from * around, join in 3rd ch of beg ch-3.

Rnds 33–35: Ch 3, fpdc around post of each fpdc and bpdc around post of each bpdc around, join in 3rd ch of beg ch-3. At end of last rnd, turn.

Rnd 36: Ch 1, (sc, ch 5, sc) in first st and in each st around, join in first sc. Fasten off.

Turn cuff down.

For pompom, wrap pink 50 times around cardboard, slide lps off cardboard, tie separate strand around middle of all lps; cut lps. Trim ends.

Sew pompom to rnd 6 on front of foot.

October

Ribbon Pin

DESIGN BY **SUSAN LOWMAN**

SKILL LEVEL ■■■□ INTERMEDIATE

FINISHED SIZE
2 x 3 inches

MATERIALS
- Aunt Lydia's Classic Crochet size 10 crochet cotton (white: 400 yds per ball; solids: 350 yds per ball):
  10 yds #1 white
  5 yds #401 orchid pink
  1 yd #493 French rose
- Size 7/1.65mm steel crochet hook or size needed to obtain gauge
- Beading needle
- Size 8 glass beads by Mill Hill: 30 #18010 ice
- 1-inch pin back
- Craft glue

GAUGE
Ribbon: 4 sts = ½ inch; 8 rows = 2 inches

Backing: Rnds 1–3 = 1⅜ inches in diameter

PATTERN NOTES
Chain-3 at beginning of row or round counts as first double crochet unless otherwise stated.

Join with slip stitch as indicated unless otherwise stated.

RIBBON
Row 1: With orchid pink, ch 6, dc in 4th ch from hook (*first 3 chs count as first dc*), hdc in next ch, sc in last ch, turn.

Row 2: Ch 1, sc in first st, hdc in next st, dc in each of last 2 sts, turn.

Rows 3–26: Ch 3 (*see Pattern Notes*), dc in each st across, turn.

Row 27: Ch 3, dc in next st, hdc in next st, sc in last st, turn.

Row 28: Ch 1, sc in first st, hdc in next st, dc in each of last 2 sts. Fasten off.

BACKING
Rnd 1: With white, ch 4, sl st in first ch to form ring, ch 1, 8 sc in ring, **join** (*see Pattern Notes*) in beg sc. (*8 sc*)

Rnd 2: Ch 4 (*counts as first dc and ch-1*), dc in same st as beg ch-4, (dc, ch 1, dc) in each st around, join in 3rd ch of beg ch-4.

Rnd 3: Sl st in first ch sp, ch 5 (*counts as first dc and ch-2*), dc in same ch sp as beg ch-5, ch 1, [(dc, ch 2, dc) in next ch sp, ch 1] around, join in 3rd ch of beg ch-5. (*16 ch sps*)

Rnd 4: Sl st in first ch sp, ch 1, sc in same ch sp, [ch 3, sc in next ch sp] around, ch 1, join with hdc in beg sc, forming last ch sp.

Rnd 5: Ch 1, sc in this ch sp, *(dc, {ch 1, dc} 3 times) in next ch sp**, sc in next ch sp, rep from * around, ending last rep at **, join in beg sc. Fasten off.

BEADS
Sew 1 bead in each ch-1 sp between dc on rnd 5 of Backing.

FINISHING
Fold Ribbon as shown in photo.

Place Ribbon on Backing with center of overlapped Ribbon in center of Backing.

BOW
Insert French rose thread through center of Ribbon and Backing from front to back and from back to front. Tie center of thread into knot on front.

Make slip knot next to tied knot and ch 30 on each end of thread.

Tie chs in bow. Shorten 1 ch if necessary.

String 3 beads onto end of each ch. Tie end in knot to secure bead. Trim ends.

Sew or glue pin back to back of Backing just above center.

Acorn
Moccasins

DESIGN BY **DARLA SIMS**

SKILL LEVEL ■■■□ INTERMEDIATE

FINISHED SIZES

Instructions given for woman's shoe sizes 5 and 6 (small) 9 inches, sizes 7 and 8 (medium) 9½ inches and sizes 9 and 10 (large) 10 inches.

Instructions given for man's shoe sizes 5 and 6 (X-small) 9 inches, sizes 7 and 8 (small) 9½ inches, size 9 (medium) 10 inches, sizes 10 and 11 (large) 10½ inches.

MATERIALS

- NaturallyCaron.com Country medium (worsted) weight yarn (3 oz/185 yds/85g per skein):
  2 [2, 4] skeins #0020 loden forest
  1 oz/50 yds/28g each #0019 vicuna and #0015 deep taupe
- Size crochet hook needed for size and gauge with men's sizes in red
- Size E/4/3.5mm crochet hook
- Required size adhesive grippers
- Tapestry needle
- Stitch marker

GAUGE

Size G/6/4mm crochet hook (small/ X-small): 14 sts = 4 inches

Size H/8/5mm crochet hook (medium/ small): 12 sts = 4 inches

Size I/9/5.5mm crochet hook (large/ medium): 10 sts = 4 inches

Size J/10/6mm crochet hook (large): 8 sts = 4 inches

PATTERN NOTES

Attach adhesive grippers to the bottom of the slippers for traction.

Hold 2 strands together throughout unless otherwise stated.

Join with slip stitch as indicated unless otherwise stated.

Work in continuous rounds, do not turn or join unless otherwise stated.

Mark first stitch of each round.

Chain-3 at beginning of row or round counts as first half double crochet and chain-1 unless otherwise stated.

Continued

Chain-2 at beginning of row or round counts as first half double crochet unless otherwise stated.

MOCCASIN
MAKE 2.

SOLE
Rnd 1: With loden forest and **2 strands held together** (*see Pattern Notes*), ch 25, 3 sc in 2nd ch from hook, sc in each of next 10 chs, dc in each of next 12 chs, 5 dc in last ch, working on opposite side of ch, dc in each of next 12 chs, sc in each of next 10 chs, 2 sc in last ch, **do not join** (*see Pattern Notes*). (54 sts)

Rnd 2: 2 sc in each of first 2 sts, sc in each of next 23 sts, 2 sc in each of next 5 sts, sc in each of next 23 sts, 2 sc in last st. (62 sts)

Rnd 3: Sc in first st, 3 sc in next st, sc in each of next 25 sts, 2 sc in next st, [sc in next st, 2 sc in next st] 4 times, sc in each of next 25 sts, 2 sc in last st. (70 sts)

Rnd 4: Sc in each of first 20 sts, dc in each of next 34 sts, sc in each of last 16 sts, **join** (*see Pattern Notes*) in **back lp** (*see Stitch Guide*) of next st.

SIDE
Rnd 1: Working in back lps, sc in each st around, join in beg sc.

Rnds 2–8: Ch 1, sc in each st around, join in beg sc. At end of last rnd, fasten off.

INSTEP
Row 1: Beg at toe, join loden forest, ch 4, sc in 2nd ch from hook and in each of last 2 chs, turn. (3 sc)

Row 2: Ch 1, 2 sc in first st, sc in next st, 2 sc in last st, turn. (5 sc)

Row 3: Ch 1, sc in each st across, turn.

Row 4: Ch 1, 2 sc in first st, sc in each of next 3 sts, 2 sc in last st, turn. (7 sc)

Row 5: Ch 1, sc in each st across, turn.

Row 6: Ch 1, 2 sc in first st, sc in each of next 5 sts, 2 sc in last st, turn. (9 sc)

Rows 7–15: Ch 1, sc in each st across, turn.

Row 16: Ch 1, sc in first st, dc in each of next 7 sts, sc in last st, turn.

Row 17: Ch 1, sk first st, sc in next st, dc in each of next 5 sts, sc in next st, sl st in last st. Fasten off.

ASSEMBLY
Turn Moccasin inside out. With RS of Moccasin facing, sew Instep in place. Turn RS out.

EDGING
Rnd 1: Join 1 strand of loden forest with sc at center back, sc in each st around, with 2 sc in each center 5 sts of Instep only, join in beg sc.

Rnd 2: Working from left to right, ch 1, **reverse sc** (*see Stitch Guide*) in each st around, join in beg reverse sc. Fasten off.

ACORN
MAKE 2.

Rnd 1: With E hook and 1 strand vicuna, leaving long end, ch 2, 6 sc in 2nd ch from hook, do not join. (6 sc)

Rnd 2: Sc in each st around.

Rnd 3: 2 sc in each st around. (12 sc)

Rnd 4: Sc in each st around, join in beg sc. Fasten off.

Rnd 5: Leaving long end, join deep taupe with sc in first st, tr in next st, [sc in next st, tr in next st] around.

Rnd 6: [**Sc dec** (*see Stitch Guide*) in next 2 sts] around, join in beg sc. Leaving long end, fasten off.

Stuff long end at beg inside Acorn.

Weave long end at end of last rnd through top of sts, pull to close. Secure end.

STEM
Join deep taupe in top of 1 Acorn, ch 10, sl st in top of rem Acorn, sl st in first ch of ch-10, sl st in each ch across, sl st in beg sl st. Fasten off.

Sew center of Stem to front of Moccasin as shown in photo.

December

Christmas Pineapple Afghan

DESIGNED BY **JUDY TEAGUE TREECE**

SKILL LEVEL ◼◼◼▢ INTERMEDIATE

FINISHED SIZE
53½ x 66½ inches

MATERIALS
- Red Heart Super Saver medium (worsted) weight yarn (7 oz/364 yds/198g per skein) 7 skeins #390 hot red
- Size H/8/5mm crochet hook or size needed to obtain gauge
- Tapestry needle

GAUGE
Rnds 1–3 of Block = 3¾ inches across

Each Block is 13 inches square

PATTERN NOTES
Chain-4 at beginning of round counts as first double crochet and chain-1 unless otherwise stated.

Continued

Chain-3 at beginning of round counts as first double crochet unless otherwise stated.

Join with slip stitch as indicated unless otherwise stated.

SPECIAL STITCH
Point: (Sc, hdc, dc, tr, dc, hdc, sc) in next st.

BLOCK
Make 20.

Rnd 1: Ch 4, sl st in first ch to form ring, **ch 4** *(see Pattern Notes)*, [dc in ring, ch 1] 7 times, **join** *(see Pattern Notes)* in 3rd ch of beg ch-4. *(8 dc, 8 ch sps)*

Rnd 2: (Sl st, ch 4, dc) in first ch sp, ch 3, sc in next ch sp, ch 3, *(dc, ch 1, dc) in next ch sp, ch 3, sc in next ch sp, ch 3,rep from * around, join in 3rd ch of beg ch-4. *(12 ch sps)*

Rnd 3: (Sl st, ch 1, sc, ch 6, sc) in first ch sp, *ch 2, (dc, ch 1, dc) in next ch sp, ch 1, (dc, ch 1, dc) in next ch sp, ch 2** (sc, ch 6, sc) in next ch sp, rep from * around, ending last rep at **, join in first sc. *(24 ch sps)*

Rnd 4: (Sl st, **ch 3**—*see Pattern Notes*, 8 dc) in first ch sp, *ch 2, sk next 2 ch sps, (dc, ch 1, dc) in next ch sp, ch 2, sk next 2 ch sps**, 9 dc in next ch sp, rep from * around, ending last rep at **, join 3rd ch of beg ch-3.

Rnd 5: Ch 4, dc in next dc, [ch 1, dc in next dc] 7 times, *ch 2, sk next ch sp, (dc, ch 2, dc) in next ch sp, ch 2, sk next ch sp**, dc in next dc, [ch 1, dc in next dc] 8 times, rep from * around, ending last rep at ** join 3rd ch of ch-4.

Rnd 6: (Sl st, ch 1, sc) in first ch sp, *ch 2, [sc in next ch sp, ch 2] 7 times, sk next ch sp, (dc, ch 1, dc, ch 1, dc) in next ch sp, ch 2, sk next ch sp**, sc in next ch sp, rep from * around, ending last rep at **, join in first sc.

Rnd 7: (Sl st, ch 1, sc) in first ch sp, *ch 2, [sc in next ch sp, ch 2] 5 times, sc in next ch sp, ch 3, sk next ch sp, (dc, ch 1, dc) in next ch sp, ch 2, (dc, ch 1, dc) in next ch sp, ch 3, sk next ch sp**, sc in next ch sp, rep from * around, ending last rep at **, join in beg sc.

Rnd 8: (Sl st, ch 1, sc) in first ch sp, *ch 2, [sc in next ch sp, ch 2] 4 times, sc in next ch sp, ch 3, sk next ch sp, (dc, ch 1, dc) in each of next 3 ch sps, ch 3, sk next ch sp**, sc in next ch sp, rep from * around, ending last rep at **, join in beg sc.

Rnd 9: (Sl st, ch 1, sc) in first ch sp, *ch 2, [sc in next ch sp, ch 2] 3 times, sc in next ch sp, ch 3, sk next ch sp, (dc, ch 1, dc) in next ch sp, (ch 2, dc, ch 1, dc) in each of next 2 ch sps, ch 3, sk next ch sp**, sc in next ch sp, rep from * around, ending last rep at **, join in beg sc.

Rnd 10: (Sl st, ch 1, sc) in first ch sp, *[ch 2, sc in next ch sp] 3 times, ch 4, sk next ch sp, (dc, ch 1, dc) in each of next 5 ch sps, ch 4, sk next ch sp**, sc in next ch sp, rep from * around, ending last rep at **, join in beg sc.

Rnd 11: (Sl st, ch 1, sc) in first ch sp, *[ch 2, sc in next ch sp] twice, ch 4, sk next ch sp, (dc, ch 1, dc) in next ch sp, (ch 2, dc, ch 1, dc) in each of next 4 ch sps, ch 4, sk next ch sp**, sc in next ch sp, rep from * around, ending last rep at **, join in beg sc.

Rnd 12: (Sl st, ch 1, sc) in first ch sp, *ch 2, sc in next ch sp, ch 4, sk next ch sp, 2 dc in each of next 4 ch sps, (2 dc, ch 2, 2 dc) in next ch sp, 2 dc in each of next 4 ch sps, ch 4, sk next ch sp**, sc in next ch sp, rep from * around, ending last rep at **, join in beg sc.

Rnd 13: (Sl st, ch 1, sc) in first ch sp, *ch 4, sk next ch sp, dc in each of next 10 dc, (2 dc, ch 2, 2 dc) in next ch sp, dc in each of next 10 dc, ch 4, sk next ch sp**, sc in next ch sp, rep from * around, ending last rep at **, join in beg sc.

Rnd 14: Sl st in first ch sp, ch 4 *(counts as first tr)*, 3 tr in same sp as beg ch-4, *dc in each of next 12 dc, (2 dc, ch 2, 2 dc) in next ch sp, dc in each of next 12 dc**, 4 tr in each of next 2 ch sps, rep from * around, ending last rep at **, 4 tr in last ch sp, join in 4th ch of beg ch-4. Fasten off. *(36 sts across each side between corner ch sps)*

Holding Blocks RS tog, matching sts, working through both thicknesses and in **back lps** *(see Stitch Guide)*, sc tog in 4 rows of 5 Blocks each.

EDGING
Working around entire outer edge, join red with sc in any corner ch sp, •◊*[sc in next 2 sts, work **point** *(see Special Stitches)*, (sc in next 4 sts, work point) 6 times, sc in next 3 sts], sk next seam], rep from * across to last Block on this side, rep between [ ] once•, sc in next corner ch sp◊; rep between ◊ twice, rep between • once, join in beg sc. Fasten off.

Stitch Guide

ABBREVIATIONS

beg	begin/begins/beginning
bpdc	back post double crochet
bpsc	back post single crochet
bptr	back post treble crochet
CC	contrasting color
ch(s)	chain(s)
ch-	refers to chain or space previously made (e.g., ch-1 space)
ch sp(s)	chain space(s)
cl(s)	cluster(s)
cm	centimeter(s)
dc	double crochet (singular/plural)
dc dec	double crochet 2 or more stitches together, as indicated
dec	decrease/decreases/decreasing
dtr	double treble crochet
ext	extended
fpdc	front post double crochet
fpsc	front post single crochet
fptr	front post treble crochet
g	gram(s)
hdc	half double crochet
hdc dec	half double crochet 2 or more stitches together, as indicated
inc	increase/increases/increasing
lp(s)	loop(s)
MC	main color
mm	millimeter(s)
oz	ounce(s)
pc	popcorn(s)
rem	remain/remains/remaining
rep(s)	repeat(s)
rnd(s)	round(s)
RS	right side
sc	single crochet (singular/plural)
sc dec	single crochet 2 or more stitches together, as indicated
sk	skip/skipped/skipping
sl st(s)	slip stitch(es)
sp(s)	space/spaces/spaced
st(s)	stitch(es)
tog	together
tr	treble crochet
trtr	triple treble
WS	wrong side
yd(s)	yard(s)
yo	yarn over

Chain—ch: Yo, pull through lp on hook.

Slip stitch—sl st: Insert hook in st, pull through both lps on hook.

Single crochet—sc: Insert hook in st, yo, pull through st, yo, pull through both lps on hook.

Front post stitch—fp: Back post stitch—bp: When working post st, insert hook from right to left around post of st on previous row.

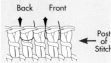

Back   Front

← Post of Stitch

Front loop—front lp Back loop—back lp

Front Loop   Back Loop

Half double crochet— hdc: Yo, insert hook in st, yo, pull through st, yo, pull through all 3 lps on hook.

Double crochet—dc: Yo, insert hook in st, yo, pull through st, [yo, pull through 2 lps] twice.

Double treble crochet— dtr: Yo 3 times, insert hook in st, yo, pull through st, [yo, pull through 2 lps] 4 times.

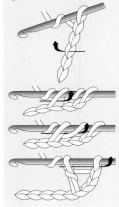

Change colors: Drop first color; with 2nd color, pull through last 2 lps of st.

Treble crochet—tr: Yo twice, insert hook in st, yo, pull through st, [yo, pull through 2 lps] 3 times.

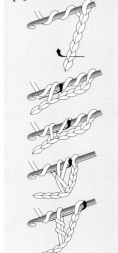

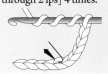

Single crochet decrease (sc dec): (Insert hook, yo, draw lp through) in each of the sts indicated, yo, draw through all lps on hook.

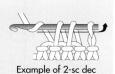

Example of 2-sc dec

Half double crochet decrease (hdc dec): (Yo, insert hook, yo, draw lp through) in each of the sts indicated, yo, draw through all lps on hook.

Example of 2-hdc dec

Double crochet decrease (dc dec): (Yo, insert hook, yo, draw lp through, yo, draw through 2 lps on hook) in each of the sts indicated, yo, draw through all lps on hook.

Example of 2-dc dec

Treble crochet decrease (tr dec): Holding back last lp of each st, tr in each of the sts indicated, yo, pull through all lps on hook.

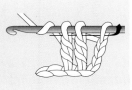

US		UK
sl st (slip stitch)	=	sc (single crochet)
sc (single crochet)	=	dc (double crochet)
hdc (half double crochet)	=	htr (half treble crochet)
dc (double crochet)	=	tr (treble crochet)
tr (treble crochet)	=	dtr (double treble crochet)
dtr (double treble crochet)	=	ttr (triple treble crochet)
skip	=	miss

For more complete information, visit

AnniesCatalog.com/ StitchGuide

Metric Conversion Charts

METRIC CONVERSIONS

yards	x .9144	=	metres (m)
yards	x 91.44	=	centimetres (cm)
inches	x 2.54	=	centimetres (cm)
inches	x 25.40	=	millimetres (mm)
inches	x .0254	=	metres (m)

centimetres	x .3937	=	inches
metres	x 1.0936	=	yards

INCHES INTO MILLIMETRES & CENTIMETRES (Rounded off slightly)

inches	mm	cm	inches	cm	inches	cm	inches	cm
1/8	3	0.3	5	12.5	21	53.5	38	96.5
1/4	6	0.6	5 1/2	14	22	56	39	99
3/8	10	1	6	15	23	58.5	40	101.5
1/2	13	1.3	7	18	24	61	41	104
5/8	15	1.5	8	20.5	25	63.5	42	106.5
3/4	20	2	9	23	26	66	43	109
7/8	22	2.2	10	25.5	27	68.5	44	112
1	25	2.5	11	28	28	71	45	114.5
1 1/4	32	3.2	12	30.5	29	73.5	46	117
1 1/2	38	3.8	13	33	30	76	47	119.5
1 3/4	45	4.5	14	35.5	31	79	48	122
2	50	5	15	38	32	81.5	49	124.5
2 1/2	65	6.5	16	40.5	33	84	50	127
3	75	7.5	17	43	34	86.5		
3 1/2	90	9	18	46	35	89		
4	100	10	19	48.5	36	91.5		
4 1/2	115	11.5	20	51	37	94		

KNITTING NEEDLES CONVERSION CHART

Canada/U.S.	0	1	2	3	4	5	6	7	8	9	10	10½	11	13	15
Metric (mm)	2	2¼	2¾	3¼	3½	3¾	4	4½	5	5½	6	6½	8	9	10

CROCHET HOOKS CONVERSION CHART

Canada/U.S.	1/B	2/C	3/D	4/E	5/F	6/G	8/H	9/I	10/J	10½/K	N
Metric (mm)	2.25	2.75	3.25	3.5	3.75	4.25	5	5.5	6	6.5	9.0

Annie's™ *Scrap Crochet Calendar 2013* is published by Annie's, 306 East Parr Road, Berne, IN 46711. Printed in USA. Copyright © 2012 Annie's. All rights reserved. This publication may not be reproduced in part or in whole without written permission from the publisher.

RETAIL STORES: If you would like to carry this publication or any other Annie's publications, visit AnniesWSL.com.

Every effort has been made to ensure that the instructions in this pattern book are complete and accurate. We cannot, however, take responsibility for human error, typographical mistakes or variations in individual work. Please visit AnniesCustomerCare.com to check for pattern updates.

ISBN: 978-1-59635-645-0

1 2 3 4 5 6 7 8 9